CIRENC[ESTER]
PARISH C[HURCH]

— A Welcome From The Vicar —

Britain's churches provide a great attraction for visitors from many parts of the world. We are pleased to welcome you to one of the largest parish churches in the country, justly described in Samuel Rudder's history of Cirencester as 'a magnificent and sumptuous building'. The graceful, lofty tower dominates the town, making a positive statement about God being at the centre of human life, with worship as the highest of human activities.

As you walk round the church, we hope that, in addition to the interesting architectural and historical features, you will appreciate that this is a lively place of daily Christian worship and prayer as well as a centre for ministry within this community.

I also hope that, during your visit, you will experience something of the special atmosphere of prayer and tranquillity which hallows these stones and speaks to us so powerfully of the presence, peace and love of God.

Hedley Ringrose

CANON HEDLEY RINGROSE

A 'Wool' Church

Gloucestershire's largest parish church looks southward across the market place, hub of the historic town's prosperity. To the north of the church is the walled precinct of the former Augustinian monastery, founded by Henry I in 1117. There are few documents to help interpret its building history, and to answer questions such as 'When was it begun?' we must look at its structure.

It is probable that after the abbey had been founded, partly on the site of a Saxon church, a new parish church was commenced, a relic of which exists in the form of a late Norman doorway in the north wall of the Lady Chapel. There is evidence of an early 13th-century rebuilding of the chancel and of the nave, but the most substantial part of the church dates from the 15th and 16th centuries.

Cirencester, along with other 'wool churches', is thus a building of mainly late medieval design. No one is certain who paid for the church or why it was so large in a town of only 2,500 people. There were ten wool merchants in mid 14th-century Cirencester and the abbey had extensive flocks of sheep. The coats of arms in the nave are mainly of nobles and of the abbey, whose arms appear above the doorway into the tower. The arms of Edmund Tame along with three or four merchant marks and a brass of a wool merchant suggest that merchants met some of the cost.

The relationship of the town with the abbey was not a happy one. The townsfolk found it particularly galling that the conduct of their trade was firmly in the hands of the Abbot.

However, when it came to church building, the monastic community made generous contributions, enabling the provision of a substantial church.

The church fabric also teaches us something about medieval politics. The most notable event to take place in Cirencester market place was the arrest and execution of two half-brothers of the deposed Yorkist king, Richard II. Approved by the new king, Henry IV of Lancaster, this action relieved the town from some of the abbey's demands and

BELGIUM: ⑤
The market place in the 19th century, from a lithograph by John Beauchamp.

Indirectly, the Romans were responsible for the tower almost collapsing before it was built. Around 1405, when the walls were only half way up, cracks began to appear. On investigation, it transpired that the foundations had been dug into a filled-in Roman ditch running alongside Ermine Street, and the earth was now settling. To combat this, the huge spur buttresses that we see today were incorporated as an emergency measure.

secured funds for the building of a great west tower.

The Trinity Chapel, begun some 50 years later in the mid 15th century, suggests by its portrait head of Richard, Duke of York (father of Richard III) that the citizens had switched allegiance. Perhaps it was this astuteness that enabled them to wheedle church building funds from their neighbour and adversary, the Abbot.

Between 1539 and 1540 the abbey was dissolved. In later years nearly all of the church's medieval furnishings, with the exception of the pulpit and parts of the screen, were destroyed.

ABOVE:
The imposing tower was built in 1400 with money received as a result of Cirencester's support for the House of Lancaster in the Wars of the Roses.

LEFT: ⑤
A very ancient Saxon crucifix of unknown origin. Now to be seen in Lady Chapel, it stands four-square with every face visible.

The Church Bells

St John's has had bells in its church tower since at least 1499. In 1722 the ring was augmented to 12 bells, one of the first in the country to have this many. It was almost 100 years before any other church in the Gloucester diocese could match this. In 1984–85 the bell frame was replaced and a new bell added. The clock was installed in 1870. Its carillon sounds every three hours with the hymn tune 'O Faith of England'.

The Nave

LEFT: ⑨
The Boleyn Cup, beautifully made of silver gilt, is one of few surviving pre-Reformation religious treasures. It was made for Anne Boleyn in 1535, the year before her execution. Her daughter Queen Elizabeth I gave it to her physician, Richard Master, who in turn gave it to Cirencester parish church.

ABOVE: ②
The 14th-century font, removed during the 18th century, was found in the abbey grounds and restored to the church in 1865.

Between 1515 and 1530 the nave was reconstructed in the Perpendicular style to replace the Early English nave of 1240 which preceded it. This in turn had replaced the Norman building. Traces of Norman work can be seen by the marks of the roof lines on the west ends of the north and south aisles.

The nave of the Perpendicular church is almost square in shape and 17 metres from floor to ceiling. Natural light floods through the great clear glass windows of the north and south walls and the high clerestory windows.

The new nave took 15 years to build, the work being paid for by the wealthy wool merchants of the town, whose crests adorn the pillars. As with most medieval churches, the walls of the nave were painted in glowing colours, but during the Reformation they were scraped off or whitewashed over.

After the destruction of the abbey in 1540, enthusiasm for the church waned and the town grew poorer. A wall was built across the nave where the font now stands. The space created served as a meeting place and the town's fire engine was kept under the tower!

A Cirencester Rarity

King James II succeeded his Stuart brother Charles II in 1685, only to be deposed after three years of unrest and persecution. The Stuart coat of arms was ordered to be destroyed throughout the land. In Cirencester, they just painted the Hanoverian arms on canvas and nailed it over the old, perhaps as a precaution against a successful Jacobite rebellion. Discovered by accident, the rare Stuart arms can now be seen once more at the eastern end of the north aisle.

Almost all of the church's medieval glass has gone, not smashed by Puritans, but through neglect of the leadwork that fixed pieces of coloured glass together.

After the restoration of Charles II in 1660, church life grew stronger. The unsightly wall was removed and galleries were built in the nave so that congregations of more than 1,200 people could be accommodated.

But by the mid 19th century major structural work was urgently needed and Sir George Gilbert Scott was called in. Under his direction, a complete renovation took place between 1865 and 1867. Once the galleries and high box pews were removed, it was clear that the many past burials under the church floor had seriously weakened the foundations of the pillars. These were reinforced and the human remains revealed were interred in the crypt under the Lady Chapel, which was sealed. The nave aisles were repaired with red tiles and new oak pews were made, the pew ends copied from a medieval original.

LEFT:
The pews occupy a large area because extra seating was required when the galleries were removed. Holy Trinity Church, Watermoor was also built to accommodate displaced worshippers.

ABOVE:
The pulpit, dating from c.1440, is one of the few medieval items to survive the Reformation. Reclaimed in 1865, it is unique in its open stonework and looks much as it did when it was built.

⑦

In the Civil War, Cirencester was staunchly for Parliament. A 1642 skirmish with Royalists resulted in defeat and over 1,000 townsmen were imprisoned in the nave overnight with no food or water before being marched to Oxford to seek pardon from Charles I.

Important Dates

*c.*300	First church in Roman town of Corinium.
577	Church and town burnt by Saxons.
*c.*700	Saxon church built.
1117	Henry I founded Abbey of St Mary. Saxon church demolished. Norman church built on present site.
1235–50	Nave rebuilt. Chancel extended. Lady Chapel built.
1400	Work on tower began.
1500	Town Hall built.
1515–30	Nave rebuilt.
1539–40	Abbey dissolved and demolished.
1865–67	Complete restoration under Sir George Gilbert Scott.
1965–1987	Major restoration of roofs and fabric.

The Chancel and The Chapels

The chancel, where the worship of the church has been offered for more than 800 years, was built in 1115 when it was both narrower and shorter than it is now. About 1180 it was widened to the south, thus throwing it out of centre with the nave. Later, in about 1240, it was extended eastward to its present length, and the arches on the south side were opened, the original columns remaining in position, the eastern one being in fact of Roman origin.

To improve visibility within, the east window was enlarged from three to five lights in 1300. The 15th and 16th-century glass was renovated and placed in position in the 20th century.

The clerestory windows in the north wall, formerly admitting light to the

RIGHT: ⑥
The fan vaulting of St Catherine's Chapel did not originally belong there. It was donated to the church, possibly having been removed from the ruins of the nearby abbey.

BELOW: ⑥
St Catherine's Chapel. A fresco of St Christopher, one of three other saints to whom the chapel was formerly dedicated, can be seen on the north wall.

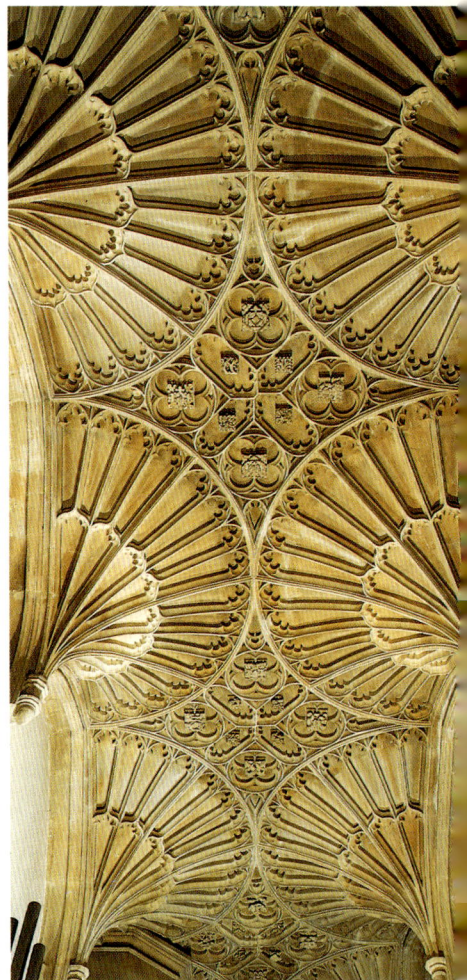

chancel, were lost when the roof of St Catherine's Chapel was raised to accommodate the fan vaulting. The arches had already been opened in 1420 and while work was in progress, the wall was underpinned, with the result that the upper wall of the chapel is older than the columns and arches now supporting it.

The sanctuary was redesigned by Sir George Gilbert Scott during the general restoration of the church in the 19th century. The fine stone reredos was designed by his son.

St Catherine's Chapel

The chapel began as the north aisle of the chancel, probably separated by a low arcade. Originally it extended only as far as the present altar rail. It is dedicated to four saints, Catherine, Christopher, Nicholas and Anthony. St Catherine was martyred on a burning wheel (hence the name of the firework) and is depicted on the south wall and again in the reredos and east window.

On the north wall is a mural of St Christopher, a big black-bearded man with the boy Christ on his shoulder. The background is red ochre, so presumably all the stone of the chapel was once this colour. The reredos, from Oberammergau, also includes St Christopher.

On the screen on the north wall was a statue of St Nicholas on a small plinth, and beneath it his altar. The medieval priest said Mass daily and the six altars in this church were fully manned (presumably by priests from the adjoining abbey). The celebrants liked to perform their duties in unison, and so from the high altar visual contact was made by narrow slits in the masonary, known as squints. The priests at St John's and St Nicholas's altars could see the high altar. The St Nicholas altar could be seen by the St Catherine and Lady Chapel celebrants, while the Trinity Chapel priest had clear contact with the Lady Chapel. Thus through four squints or 'hagioscopes', six priests could keep perfect time together.

The beautiful fan vaulting of the chapel is not an original fit, but came as a gift after the Dissolution, probably from the neighbouring abbey.

North of the altar is a canopied aumbry where the blessed sacrament is reserved for use when Communion is given in home visits.

Visitors are asked to be especially quiet in the chapel, which is kept for private prayer.

The Lady Chapel

The Lady Chapel was added around 1240 at the time when the nave was first rebuilt. A statuette of the Blessed Virgin Mary is situated to the south of the altar. It was a gift made for its niche as a thanksgiving for the end of World War II. The central passageway is carpeted to protect the brasses on the gravestones beneath. Inside the altar rails are brasses already damaged by time.

The chapel is dominated by the magnificent Bridges tomb. The carvings of Humphrey Bridges, an early 17th-century lawyer, his wife and eleven children, are beautifully and imaginatively done. Humphrey looks sober, devout and reverent above his clasped hands, while his wife seems warm-hearted, loving and humorous.

By contrast the tomb opposite of John Master, a late 17th-century lofty and dignified gentleman, suggests some change in religious thought in around 100 years. Over the small Norman arch from the Catherine Chapel is a very faded mural of the Judgement – a cartload of lost souls being pitchforked into hell by the devil.

BELOW: ⑤
The Lady Chapel, showing on the left the tomb of the Bridges family.

RIGHT: ⑤
A lime-wood statuette of the Blessed Virgin Mary, from the Lady Chapel.

The Trinity Chapel

This chantry chapel, originally for the saying of Masses for the kings and queens of England, has gone through many vicissitudes. After Edward VI abolished chantries it was disused, later becoming merely a route to one of the 18th-century galleries.

A small square stone marked by a coronetted letter 'B' is the ancient entrance to the Bathurst family crypt. Behind the altar are brasses collected from tombs all round the church, among them that of Ralph Parsons, a chantry priest who died in 1478. Remarkably his cope is still preserved under the south-west window of the nave. The chapel was founded by Sir Richard Dixton and Sir William Prelatte of the household of the Duke of York,

who in 1455 played a big part in the start of the Wars of the Roses. From an earlier window his head alone has been preserved for the central panel of the east window.

In a modern window to the north of the chapel the martyred St Stephen is shown, rather quaintly, with one of the stones that slew him carefully balanced on his head!

The carved Christ over the altar is at the centre of many empty niches long unoccupied. The Christ was carved by Sir George Gilbert Scott's son.

St Edmund's Chantry Chapel

This magnificently carved chantry chapel has links with Lancashire through a wool merchant, Henry Garstang, who in 1464 was buried in it. His arms are above the recess in the south wall in which he lies. Originally dedicated to St Edmund of Canterbury, today the chapel is used annually for an impressive Christmas crib.

Adjoining St Edmund's Chantry Chapel is a chapel dedicated to St John the Baptist. Now used as a vestry, it contains the fine tomb of George Monox, Sheriff of London in the time of Charles I. The 19th-century windows show scenes from the life of John the Baptist.

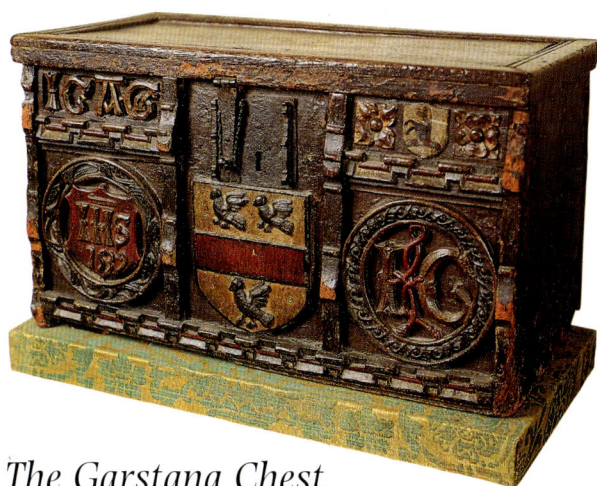

The Garstang Chest

A beautiful marriage chest dated 1539 from St Edmund's Chantry, now usually known as the Garstang Chapel. The chest stands in a recess and bears the coat of arms of the George family, whose patent dates from 1528. The family was prominent in the town for two centuries and the same arms can be seen above the altar on the east wall of the chapel. In 1722 a member of the family, Rebecca Powell, founded a charity school in the town which as a church school still bears her name.

The Parish Church Today

The unique south porch protruding into the market place is a fine historical feature and a tangible expression of the Christian Church's ministry, reaching out to the community and the world.

This three-storey Perpendicular porch was built in about the year 1490 as a meeting place outside the abbey precincts for the conduct of its secular business with the Royal Commissioners. After the Dissolution it had various functions including that of Town Hall, the name by which it is still known to townspeople. In 1671 the Bishop of Gloucester granted it to the Vicar and churchwardens for parish use.

The main room inside the Town Hall, refurbished in 1994, contains four interesting Benefaction Boards recording perpetual gifts made to the church in Cirencester. A small kitchen makes the room useful as a meeting place for a variety of church activities. During the 1990s, other developments near the church in Dollar Street have provided a new vicarage, bookshop/coffee shop – The Corner Stone – and a parish office in buildings which are themselves more than 300 years old. Strangely, the vicarage, which has at different times been in various parts of

BELOW: ⑧
A medieval carving of an angel, playing a hand organ to the glory of God.

the town, is now situated only a few yards from the original one which was demolished in 1826. A former Unitarian chapel nearby has been purchased to provide a new church hall in the town centre.

The parish of Cirencester has grown in recent years, now having a population totalling almost 20,000 people. There are two other churches in the parish: Holy Trinity, Watermoor is a fine Victorian building, built by Sir George Gilbert Scott, with a modern church hall beside it; St Lawrence Church, Chesterton is a modern dual-purpose building. Each of the churches is different in character, enabling wide-ranging styles of worship within the parish. There are also two thriving church schools, Powell's School in Gloucester Street and Watermoor School, so the Church of today seeks to serve the community and to witness to the people who live here in just the same way as it has always done.

The churchpeople of Cirencester are proud of their heritage, in buildings and in faith, so we try to share the glories of both with as many others as possible.

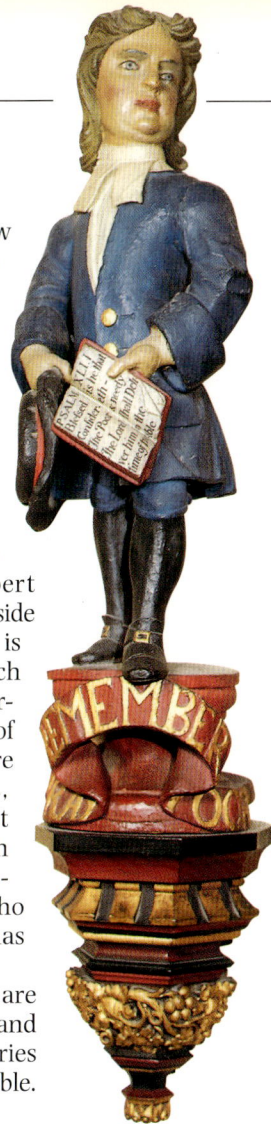

LEFT: ⑫
In Victorian times, the blue boy used to stand in the porch to beg funds for the church's schools.

FAR LEFT: ⑬
Choir members practise in the south porch, known as the Town Hall from its earlier role.

BACK COVER:
The seven-light window over the chancel arch, a feature of many Cotswold wool churches. Originally in the arch was a rood loft with the figure of Christ on the Cross, St John and the Virgin Mary being on either side. After only 25 years, in the reign of Edward VI, all roods were taken down by order. It was not until 1906 that an elaborate carved cross was hung to fill the arch once more.

Acknowledgements

The text was written by June Stacey, Stella Branston, the Revd. Martin Cooper and Canon Hedley Ringrose.
Edited by John McIlwain.
Designed by Anita Ruddell.

All photographs are © Pitkin Guides Ltd (by Peter Smith of Newbery Smith Photography) and Bryan Berkeley A.R.P.S.

Text © St John Baptist Church, Cirencester.

Publication in this form © Pitkin Guides Ltd 1997.

ISBN 0 85372 825 9   1/97

PITKIN
· GUIDES ·

THIS GUIDE IS ONE OF AN EXTENSIVE SERIES ABOUT HISTORIC PLACES AND FAMOUS PEOPLE THROUGHOUT THE BRITISH ISLES

•

Available by mail order
Write for free colour brochure and full stock list:
Pitkin Guides, Healey House, Dene Road, Andover, Hampshire, SP10 2AA, UK.
Tel: 01264 334303 Fax: 01264 334110

ISBN 0 85372 808 9
9 780853 728252